SUCCESS OF A CREATIVE AND INNOVATIVE COMPANY

SUMMARY

INTRODUCTION

I. **MARKET ANALYSIS**
    A. SWOT
    B. TRENDS PER SEGMENT
    C. COMPETITION
    D. CONSUMERS INSIGHTS

II. **MICHEL ET AUGUSTIN: BUILDING A BRAND**
    A. HISTORY
    B. MISSION AND VALUES
    C. PRODUCTS PORTFOLIO
    D. TARGET
    E. FINANCIAL RESULTS
    F. INTERNATIONALISATION OF THE BRAND

III. **A CREATIVE AND INNOVATIVE COMPANY**
    A. ENTREPRENEUR PROFILES
        a. Michel entrepreneurial ingredients
        b. Augustin entrepreneurial ingredients
        c. The final recipy: concoction of two complementary profiles
    B. A GREAT DOSE OF CREATIVITY
        a. Communication strategy: disruption
        b. An original packaging

IV. **MANAGEMENT PHILOSOPHY**
    A. MANAGEMENT STYLE
    B. HIRING PROCESS

CONCLUSION
REFERENCES
ANNEXES

INTRODUCTION

The American have their famous Ben & Jerry's, the German have Ben & Nuts and from now on, the French have their two kooky cookies: Michel et Augustin.

This French cooking-making venture is created in Paris in 2004 and 10 years later, it has become a strong brand on the French food market. On this mature market, dominated by large food-processing companies, Michel et Augustin managed to get a place through innovative products and an original way to communicate. With a value proposition non-existing on the market (playful positioning and products "homemade"), they establish a niche of loyal customers.

Michel et Augustin today is:
- Intense growth of 44%
- 21 million of products
- 78 employees
- 3 headquarters: Paris, Lyon and New-York
- 4002 job applications received

The two co-founders have created a joyful and entertaining environment in all aspects of their business: products, communication, management are part of a strong brand identity they managed to build.

This case reveals the secret ingredients of a successful business model. We are going to explain how a simple but innovative idea has made the success of a growing start-up, using the concept of "creative entrepreneurship".

MARKET ANALYSIS

The agro-food market is "mature" and is dominated by huge companies such as Danone, Nestlé, Mondelez International or Cadburry. The barriers to entry are high and competition is very strong. It is difficult for new entrants to get a place on this market and to compete the big leaders.

A. SWOT

STRENGHTS	WEAKNESSES
· Young and dynamic company · Continuous innovation · Original and creative packaging · Natural & home-made products · Funny · Original communication · Profit increase	· High prices · Lack of financial resources for communication (high budget for competitors) · Small structure
OPPORTUNITIES	**THREATHS**
· Consumers look for natural products (organic) · No competitor with the same positioning (home-made) · Demand of foreign countries	· Increase of raw material prices · Strong competition with high budgets · Economic recession, decrease of purchasing power

B. TRENDS PER SEGMENT

Sweet cookies

The cookies market has been very affected by the 2008 crisis but sales recovered since 2012. Ninety percent of products are sold in hypermarkets. Total consumption of cakes per year per capita is about 8.4 kg. Cookies and cakes are mainly consumed in the afternoon "tea time" and breakfast. They often are consumed in family. The market is changing: it is mature and saturated so innovation should be present.

	2013	2012	2008	2013/2012	2013/2008
Value	2 025 millions €	1 963 millions €	2 400 millions €	+3,2%	-18,5%
Volume	458 700 tonnes	448 400 tonnes	461 500 tonnes	+2,3%	-0,6%

Salted Crackers

The salted cakes market is very dynamic in France. The prices do not rise too much, innovation is present and consumer habits grow in snack and appetizer buffet supper. The turnover was about 1.3 billion € in France in 2013 (+ 6.2% in value vs. 2012). One French in two takes aperitif at least once a week.

Yogurt

Yogurt is the preferred dairy product of French people. A person consumes around 0.5 yogurt daily. Most of time, the consumption takes place during lunch or dinner. However, yogurt consumption tends to stagnate.

Mixed fruits

Ninety-two percent of French people consume fruit juices, 43% daily. In 2013, they consumed 1.64 billion liters. Fruit juice consumption is especially popular with adults, mainly at home (95%) and privileged during breakfast (65%). The fruit juice market is driven by government campaigns that encourage eating fruit every day.

C.   COMPETITION

Sweet cookies	Lu, Gue, Bonne Maman, Cadburry, Pepperidge Farm, Albert Mené, Barilla Mulino Bianco, Saint Michel, Brink, Delacre, Mère Poulard
Salted Crackers	Berlin, Ancel, Lu, Vico
Yogurt and dairy	Danone, Lactel, Yoplait, La Laitière, Mamie Nova, Nestle
Foam	Bonne Maman, Mamie Nova, La Laitière
Mixed fruits	Andros, Danone, Materne, Taillefine, Innocent

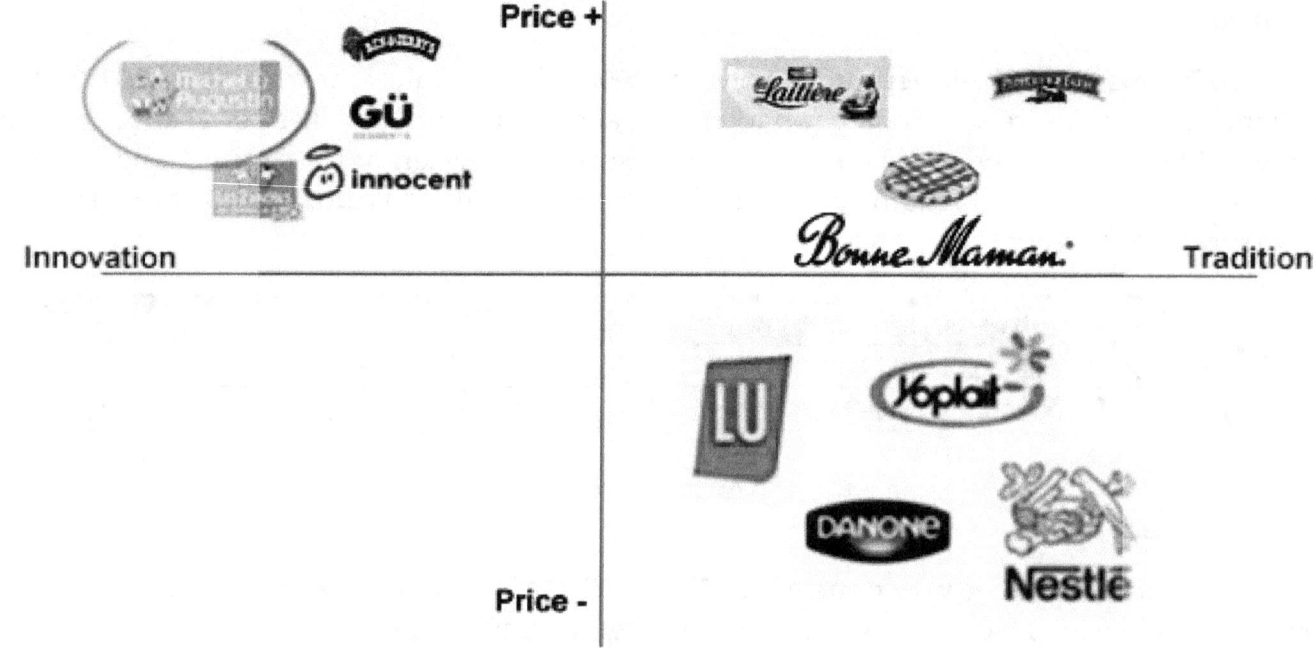

D. CONSUMERS INSIGHTS

What people need and want today when they buy a product?
→ "Home-made" trend
→ Funny products, concepts and packaging

Nowadays with the increase of mass-market products, the consumer has many choices while pacing up and down the supermarket aisles. For instance, for one cookies pack the client is looking for, it will have a proposition of about 10 brands and 30 products with different packages, flavors, sizes, prices etc. The challenge for the newcomers is thus to manage to differentiate the products from the competitors ones in an original way, because they cannot directly compete a leader such as Nestlé or Coca-Cola. They have to be visible on the store shelves being still unknown by the consumer. A key tool is the packaging and Michel et Augustin clearly understood this point.

MICHEL ET AUGUSTIN: BUILDING A BRAND

A. HISTORY

Building a brand is like cooking a cake: it takes time

These two business school students with comfortable jobs decided in 2004 to transform their passion about food into a full-time job. They started the business in Augustin's apartment with the aim to cook "sablés", a special type of cookies. In the footsteps of Ben Cohen and Jerry Greenfield, the founders of Ben & Jerry's, the two childhood friends Augustin Paluel-Marmont and Michel de Rovira created in 2005 their brand of biscuits **Michel et Augustin.** At the beginning, they sold their cookies in small shops in Paris, in the street, and more and more in the Parisian supermarkets. They distributed packets by walking or cycling. In parallel, they began their culinary adventure writing a guide to Parisian bakeries: "Le guide des boulangeries de Paris" and tested recipes in their own kitchen. In 2006, the production increased, and the company moved in a bigger site. They diversified the products line and increased the sales points.

Key dates:

2003: Drafting of Paris bakeries Guide.

2004: Creation of Michel & Augustin. : Launch of "Little Sable Round and Good" and "Fruit Drink".

2010: Launch of the "Cow Bar" at the Grande Epicerie de Paris. Michel et Augustin won the Phoenix Award for innovation and communication by the Union of advertisers, ahead Evian and McDonald's. The same year, the French brand recorded 40% growth in turnover

2011: Introduction of Michel biscuits and yoghurts And Augustin in the United States.

2013: Pinault repurchase Michel and Augustin units, the two founders retaining a 30% stake.

B. MISSION AND VALUES

- **Production**

The Bananeraie priority is in the quality of the products used to cook the delicious desserts, yogurts, biscuits, foams etc. Each morning, at 9am, the team has a meeting to taste one by one a sample of each reference of the last productions. More than 50 products are controlled each week.

Both the cookies and juices are produced with natural ingredients and no preservatives – or just a bit - as stated by Michel: "By bringing together the best ingredients, no additives or preservatives, we find the taste of our grand-mothers cookies. This is our position". However, good products also mean higher productions costs, avoiding artificial aroma, thickeners or coloring substitutes.

The company wants to focus on the quality. The products are "Made in France" and produced in different regions of the country: the rice is from Camargue, the vanilla is imported from La Réunion, they use salt from Guérande (Bretagne) and the lemons are picked in Murcia. Michel and Augustin work with small and medium companies depending on the regional specializations. Their purpose is not to promote the organic food, just the quality of the ingredients they cook with. According to Augustin, it is necessary to eat organic food, healthy products and to have a balanced diet. Michel and Augustin products surf on the new diet concept and the customers like it.

The production areas respect the health standards in force. All products have the HACCP standard, one has the IFS (International Food Standard) and others are on the way to get the certification.

- **Values**

Their main mission is to make people smile, the whole planet, especially those who do not smile anymore or not so much. How do they manage to do that? Creating, developing, living and sharing this human adventure. The tribe's values are joy of life, sport, entrepreneurship, simplicity, solidarity, sharing, health, eco-friendly mind and the sense of effort.

Keeping this state-of-mind, Michel et Augustin decided to give the benefits of their interventions and conferences to Bouée d'Espoir, an association fighting against the social exclusion. They work with a "helping center via the work" to cook the little meringues. Martin has a handicap but has been working in the company as courier for 4 years. He is fully integrated to the team and he takes care of the deliveries, using exclusively the subway.

C.   PRODUCTS PORTFOLIO

The success of Michel and Augustin is not the marketing budget. They use the product and company values with a clever policy. Cookies, yogurts, desserts and pre-dinner biscuits are only homemade and they cook with quality ingredients. The positioning is premium. Besides, the price is more expensive compared with the competitors. The first two products sold in supermarkets and fast foods under the brand name were:
- "petit sablé rond et bon" (little round and good shortbread);
- "fruits à boire" (fruits to drink)

Then the number of creations increased dramatically varying from cookies to juices, desserts and more:

Cookies:

- "Petites baguettes";
- "Super cookies coeur fondant" (soft-heart cookies);
- "Palmiers allongés" (long palmiers);
- "Mini cookies coeur fondant" (mini soft-heart cookies);
- "Petits cookies from France".

Yogurts:

- "Vache à boire"
- "Petit pot de yaourt"

Sharable desserts:
- "L'incroyable mousse".

Aperitive biscuits:
- "29 sablés apéritif ronds et bons";
- "Feuilletés apéritif croustillants et bons".

Juices:
a. "L'incroyable citronnade".

To go:
- «cookie square…actually rectangles»
- «cookie square…totally square»
- «4 cookie square sitting in the row»

D.   TARGET

The target customers of Michel et Augustin is between 15 and 25 years old, living in big cities, urban profiles with a high-purchasing power. To achieve to reach this target, the packaging is designed in an appealing childish way and in the logo are included caricatures of the two founders. For more interactivity with the customer, on the packaging, there are also telephone contacts and email addresses.

E.   FINANCIAL RESULTS

Their success increased first in France but also internationally. In 2013 Michel et Augustin reached a total turnover of 18.5 million €, whereas in 2014 they reached a turnover of 35 million. On the following graph is shown the increasing turnover of the company through the years.

TOTAL TURNOVER (MILLION EUROS) SINCE 2005

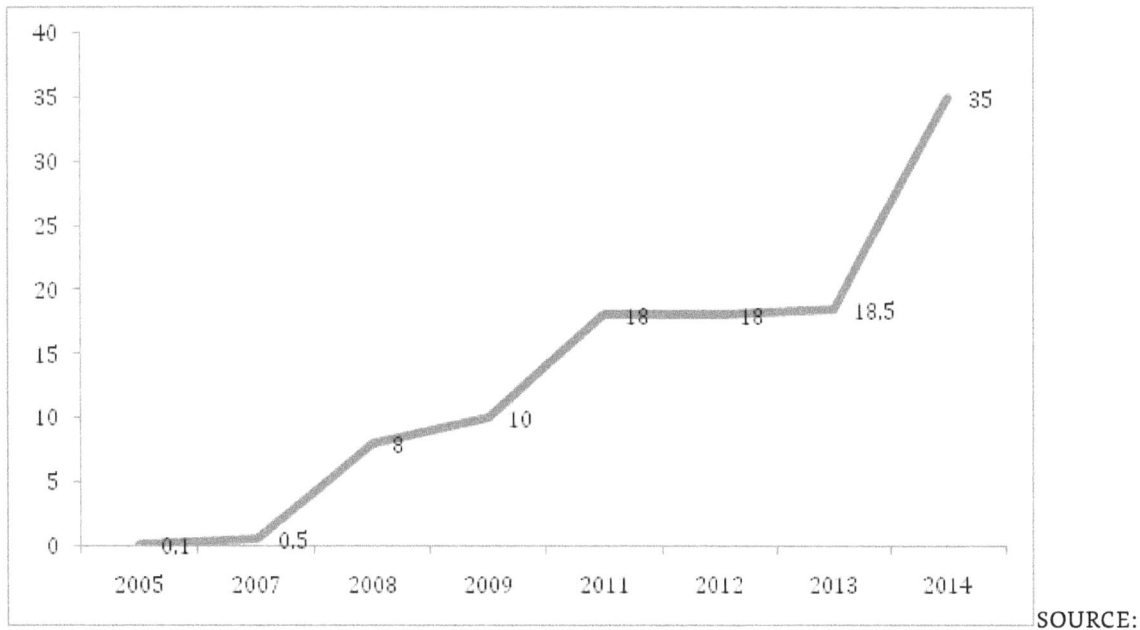

SOURCE: http://it.pictovia.com/courbes-lisses/michel-et-augustin-turnover-evolution-1431

By the time they constructed a solid base on the brand, in nine years there was a constant increase of the company total turnover (+15% since 2013), also thanks to 80 employees that work with passion inside the company. In 2012, the 70% of the total turnover was realized just in Paris, 20% in the Province region, 10% internationally. They expect to reach a turnover of 100 million € between 2016 and 2017. In terms of sales, the company reached 25 million € in 2013, enhanced at 35 million € in 2014.

Today, the company distributes its products in more than 6000 points of sales around the world. Moreover, they are oriented on sales force on the field, using the "key accounting" that might be important for high-grow firms.

In terms of distribution, they use a logistic support by an internal operation team, distributing directly to warehouses and point of sales. More precisely their circuit of distribution is GDA, E-commerce, alternative circuits, restaurants of enterprises and specialized shops.

F.   INTERNATIONALISATION OF THE BRAND

As written in the previous page, 10% of their total turnover comes from abroad sales. The main buyers are Switzerland and Belgium. In 2011, they entered in the US market after a two-year research in which they made promotion of the product by testing products in the streets of NY and asking the walkers their opinion.

After more than 8 years of existence, Michel et Augustin is already present in 15 countries including the UK, China, Hong Kong, Dubai and Canada. Moreover, with the exception of Dubai and China, they did not need to adapt their products. They export according to the 20/80 method. That is to say, they only exported products (20% of them) which generate 80% of their turnover.

To believe Antoine Chauvel, export director of Michel et Augustin, the company sees everything through rose-colored glasses and is positive about its future. The proof, in 2017, the French company aims to achieve 15 million € in turnover abroad.

A CREATIVE AND INNOVATIVE COMPANY

A. ENTREPRENEUR PROFILES

a. Michel entrepreneurial ingredients

Michel de Rovira is graduated from the ESCP-EAP French business school. He worked at LEK Consulting as a strategy consultant in the food sector and made several development missions for the US millers. He explains: "I accepted to drop his job to enter in Michel & Augustin adventure" → ***Risk taker***

As he was working as a strategy consultant, the environment was very formal. However, Michel believes that corporate culture is the basic requirement. His vision of the company is an environment where everyone gives their best keeping cohesion of the team. Michel calls himself a happy boss because his company is in good condition, his staff smiles and this makes it easier to develop new innovative projects. Today there are about 80 people in the company. For Michel is the first experience as a manager and with the company growth his managerial approach has changed, but always keeping a good dose of humility, keeping listening to his employees and learn from others without forgetting anyone → ***Motivating manager and organized***

b. Augustin entrepreneurial ingredients

Augustin Paluel-Marmont is graduated from the ESCP-EAP business school too. His first job was as an analyst in strategy for Club Méditerranée, then he co-founded a company specialized in data mining and he has been product manager in the Air France marketing division. In 2001, he took and passed a CAP-BEP in bakery.

According to the co-founder, the company's goal is to offer natural products and smile. He knew nothing about the food industry but he worked and learned hardly to know this market, its challenges, actors, trends and evolutions → ***Hard-worker and manages to open the right door of the opportunities' corridor, and hard worker***

According to him, everything someone does, even the failures are part of a professional enrichment. He is not afraid by market threats and likes challenges. In his life, he tries to be as optimistic as possible. He has energy, self-confidence and is able to learn from the surroundings → ***Risk taker, challenger and optimistic***

His basic principle is to use his imagination and not his wallet. In fact, the media tell what is going on in his company in a modern and authentic way of work. → ***Creativity***

> "I was definitely nervous, but also excited about committing to Michel et Augustin. Most of my business school friends were going to great jobs in consulting or industry, and I was considering baking. A part of me wanted to choose a 'safe' path, but another part wanted to see whether we would succeed. That part won the argument" (Michel)

The five Augustin's tips to be a good entrepreneur:
- Do not expect to have the right idea to start entrepreneurial activity, but to embark and work hard to make the idea become a good one;

- Do not listen too much to discouraging people and believe in your vision;

- Surround yourself with good people because the secret of success are those with whom you work;

- Keep tabs on your energies because we often start running too fast, but the road ahead is long;

- Life is beautiful if you are two, maintaining equality, no matter who did what.

---

c. The final recipe: concoction of two complementary profiles

Michel and Augustin met in the Parisian school "Franklin". Michel was a good student, but he had only a few problems in physics. Augustin, however, was an extrovert student who liked to play rugby, theater, to travel and who enjoyed photography. The teacher who has most marked the life of Michel is the philosophy's one. Michel was impressed by his words. Augustin had a rather difficult adolescence, but fortunately, he was helped to overcome it by a professor who was teaching French, Greek and philosophy.

Several years later, the road has been walked along. The 17th December 2014, Michel and Augustin are elected as "celebrities of the year" in the industrial PME category, at "Les Trophées LSA 2014 de l'innovation" rewarding the innovative projects, products and personalities of the year, working in the mass market, for their exemplary results.

Finally, what did they learn from their adventure? To them, two main strategic errors should not be made for a start-up launch: never believe that a company can be created in one year. That is impossible, patience and a lot of time are needed to manage a successful launch. Moreover, it is crucial to have a performing hiring process from the beginning since a good team is a key success factor.

B. A GREAT DOSE OF CREATIVITY

a. Communication strategy: disruption

Michel et Augustin implemented a different marketing strategy and made a disruption that gave them a place on a mature market in just few years. They stand as your friends: the goal is to create a familiar link with the consumer.

How to manage to enter a market with lots of competitors when you do not have the financial tools to be the "big one"? The two entrepreneurs managed to do it thanks to their communication, using principally the buzz method. This latest consists in drawing attention of people with a funny, original or provocative action and a tiny financial budget (for Michel et Augustin, 50 times lower than their competitors do). Meanwhile, it is important to filter the information given to the consumer and competitors and have an efficient gatekeeper. For instance on their website, Michel et Augustin inform of the products' nature and origin but do not reveal the secret of their recipes.

Their communication is a reflection of their spirit and their way of managing: humor, proximity and spontaneity. Not having much money to invest in traditional tools of communication, both co-founders used their creativity to make know their products from the beginning: for example, in 2005, they distribute their cookies in rollerblades in Paris, dressed like cows.

The website is the best tool to show their originality, giving all the information they want in the way they decide. They give some recipes ideas to cook with their own products, write funny captions on the product sheets, explain in details their ecofriendly policy, how they produce or invite you to come to the Bananeraie every first Thursday of each month and talk with the tribe. The website structure is interactive, visual, funny and ergonomic, designed like a game. This communication style is fully assumed by the use of a colored graphic and a childish drawings logo.

Michel et Augustin are also experts in doing "the buzz" via street Marketing operations such as the one with the "huge cow" in Paris, a big cow drawled on the banner and hung on monuments (appendices). In 2012, the "clean tag" concept consists in tagging the Parisian walls with an herbal cow. Finally, in April 2015, Michel et Augustin made the buzz by sending the human resources manager recruiting staff in the Parisian subway, an original way to hire but also an effective, simple and a costless marketing tool. The initiative is full of humor and allows the brand to get more awareness.

They are also present and active on the social networks, especially Facebook and Instagram. The brand managed to build a strong reputation around the relationship with customers and this loyalty is a critical part of their growth and success: 125 000 "like" on Facebook, about 100 000 subscribers to their newsletters, 5000 followers on Instagram and 23 000 followers on Tweeter. The consumer opinion is important and they do not hesitate to ask for some advices directly before a launch. The 4th June 2014 they publish a Facebook survey presenting the new packaging under two ranges of sharable yogurts boxes and asking to the web surfers to vote for the favorite one. They also encourage people traveling by train to post a picture of their "afternoon tea" with the "hashtag" on Instagram. The products are always connected. Customers share the product in social network. Besides, the group attracts the sympathy of the media accepting all kinds of interviews.

b. An original packaging

Michel et Augustin use funny and modern packaging to differentiate their products to "traditional" positioning of other brands. They play with colorful images and drawing shifted to be more attractive in the supermarket shelves. The customers buy an educational and recreational product; they want to create a special moment of pleasure and leisure. The packaging sometimes is transparent to incite the consumers.

The formats selected by the co-founders are also innovative on the food market. For example, they invest in large yogurt sizes to share and enjoy with the whole family. This type of packaging is less polluting for the environment. Besides, their first products, "les petits sablés" were sold in small square boxes, easy to slip into a bag or a pocket. They need less space on the shelf, so the leaders convince supermarkets to place them next to the cash register: this is good for a last minute or impulsive purchase.

For the co-founders, it is essential to have clear information on the packaging as exact names of the product components and their origin. The add value of company is use simple and known components and they find important to highlight it on the packaging.

MANAGEMENT PHILOSOPHY

A. MANAGEMENT STYLE

- **A "good mood" management**

Initially, there were only two. Today, Augustin Paluel-Marmont and Michel de Rovira lead a 70 employee's team called the "troublemakers" in their headquarters called "la bananeraie" in Paris. These fun and cheerful names match to the image of the company and to the atypical management implemented there. "The management by good mood," is their motto. The warm atmosphere, sharing and friendliness are the highlights of this management strategy and are part of the company's success. "Our customers cannot take any pleasure consuming our products if our team does not take pleasure designing them" explains Augustin Paluel-Marmont. They manage to be serious without taking itself seriously. The strength of this type of management is to make employees proud and enthusiastic working for the brand.

- **Encouraging employees to be "intrapreneurs"**

Employees are encouraged to behave like real entrepreneurs and each team takes part to the innovation adventure. Everyone can propose ideas and provide advices on the development of a new product regardless the division it belongs to. For example, the accounting group may also give its opinion about a product launch. The founders want to cultivate an "out of the box" mind, waiting for shifted ideas from their employees. The routine does not exist and the teams are constantly stimulated.

There is a real confidence for employees who can work autonomously despite an established hierarchy. However, they do not impose their leading power to the whole team. According to them, it is hard to develop innovation in a tough environment. It is important to empower employees to affirm their ideas and opinions (the company library with books dealing with self-development).

Employees are encouraged to pass the exam of the CAP pastry. The ambition is to become the leading company in the food industry where all employees possess the CAP pastry. Michel owns a CAP in pastry and Augustin have a CAP in bakery. The investment of time to do for all employees is huge, but the experience is a real professional development. Some employees have started their own business. In Michel et Augustin, they are encouraged to progress as individuals

B. HIRING PROCESS

Michel and Augustin have some questions they usually ask during an interview such as: "What choices did you make since you're 18?", "Why this direction in your life?", "Why science instead of letters?". They express a deep desire to understand the candidate choices and his scholar and professional orientation until today. The interview is a moment really important, after that, they need to be sure to know perfectly the person concerned (Question: "We do not know each other and we spend one week together in a mountain shelter. After this journey, what can I say about you?").

Recently, they hired a product manager who applied by being delivered in a DHL cardboard in Augustin's desk. Originality and creativity are a plus and valorized by the two founders. Important factors to them to call candidates are principally the motivation, the degree of enthusiasm and the time people spend to prepare their interview, their personal investment. For instance, one candidate cooked a big cake to share with the whole team, another wrote a love letter.

However, it is important for the candidate to keep in mind to make the difference between this enthusiasm to work for Michel et Augustin and the reliability and responsiveness a candidate should prove to be hired. The concept is around originality and fun but employees need to be hard working to make the enterprise follow its successful way. Augustin explains: "[...] And I think we are lucky to be very creative here but without forgetting our framework and seriousness, to be sure we reach the productivity we want because we are on a very competitive market [...] so we have to combine creativity, enthusiasm and performance. And that is what we do".

The 35 hours culture in France: a problem for entrepreneurs, normality for employees.
The Jospin government in 2000 has voted this law, proposing the reduction of working hours from 39 to 35 hours per week. To the two entrepreneurs, there is a gap between their generation and the one arriving on the labor market. The latest take it for granted while the founders discovered this new way to "work less" during their career. Thus, the apprehension of the working time question is different for the two generations. When they launched their company, they worked hard, with passion and did not care about the number of hours they worked. Sometimes, the border between private and professional life was even blurred. However, in a world now promoting the leisure, traveling and easy life, the new generation does not want to spend the whole day at work: the private life is important and should not be forgotten for the benefit of your boss. Michel et Augustin try to combine the both sides: they expect from their employee a high level of commitment while being blossoming in their everyday life at work.

Michel et Augustin hire only the most brilliant, ambitious and passionate people. Brilliant while the products are always in need of improvement, ambitious because the company must remain innovative, passionate because if a person wants to work in the food industry, he must have a passion for gastronomy.

MICHEL ET AUGUSTIN

CONCLUSION

The Parisian start-up is changing the game rules on a food market dominated by multinationals consolidated over the years.

On the French market, where consumers eat more biscuits for breakfast and snacks, Michel et Augustin has found space to offer its clients products handmade with original packaging, which we see now in the supermarket shelves, at a price above average market, but that despite the global economic crisis, are very popular among the lovers of natural products. Ten years after the Michel et Augustin's creation, the products range has expanded from cookies, desserts up to the juice, always maintaining a high standard of quality combined with the company's core values in making people smile.

With sales growing, 35 million € in 2014, Michel et Augustin is sweeping across the world and today you can buy its products in New York, Moscow and Tokyo.

The secret of success of Michel et Augustin is in their founders: Michel de Rovira and Augustin Paluel-Marmont. The two friends have rediscovered a passion for good food and this passion have made their way of life, creating what is now known as Michel et Augustin. Nevertheless, passion is not enough to compete with multinational giants; it also needs a good dose of creativity. In fact, the two entrepreneurs began in 2005 to distribute biscuits in Paris dressed as cows aboard rollerblades.

Another important factor of success is the management style adopted by Michel et Augustin: the so-called "Good Mood". A friendly way to manage a company while stimulating employees to be "intrapreneurs" in a French context where the working week is 35 hours. This is the idea of a family, working with passion. For this, also the recruitment has a fundamental role.

For the future of Michel et Augustin is expected the opening of new plants in the US and in Asia, increasing the range of products in the confectionery field and maybe a diversification from the core business. Certainly, their brand will soon become known in all corners of the planet.

REFERENCES

http://cases.insead.edu/michel-and-augustin/documents/5757-MichelAugustin-CS-EN-0-03-2014-award-w.pdf

http://www.actalia.eu/consommation-jus-fruits-en-france/

http://www.alliance7.com/wp-content/uploads/2014/04/chiffres_cles_biscuits_gateaux_2013.pdf

http://www.alliance7.com/wp-content/uploads/2014/04/chiffres_cles_biscuits_gateaux_2013.pdf

http://www.breuerconsulting.com/articles/Key%20Account%20Management.pdf

http://www.dynamique-mag.com/entrepreneur/augustin-paluel-marmont.21

http://www.dynamique-mag.com/entrepreneur/augustin-paluel-marmont.21

http://www.e-marketing.fr/Thematique/Tendances-1000/Creation-Design-10003/Breves/Packaging-participatif-chez-Michel-et-Augustin-37116.htm

http://www.e-marketing.fr/Thematique/Tendances-1000/Creation-Design-10003/Breves/Packaging-participatif-chez-Michel-et-Augustin-37116.htm

http://www.franklinparis.fr/etab/ecole/ecole.php

http://www.franklinparis.fr/etab/ecole/ecole.php

http://www.journaldunet.com/management/dossiers/050480marque/michel-et-augustin.shtml

http://www.journaldunet.com/management/dossiers/050480marque/michel-et-augustin.shtml

http://www.lasimpleagence.com/packaging/packaging/

http://www.lepoint.fr/dossiers/art-de-vivre/made-in-france/michel-et-augustin-les-enfants-terribles-de-la-bonne-bouffe-27-07-2013-1708996_1608.php

http://www.lsa-conso.fr/les-gateaux-aperitifs-sont-a-la-fete,170157

http://www.lsa-conso.fr/trophees-lsa-2014-de-l-innovation-le-palmares,195004

http://www.lsa-conso.fr/trophees-lsa-2014-de-l-innovation-le-palmares,195004

http://www.micheletaugustin.com/laventure/canards/presse/2011-10-10_Points-de-vente.pdf

http://www.micheletaugustin.com/us/ourcreations/

http://www.slideshare.net/Antoinekooky/michel-et-augustin-brand-strategy-and-products-august-2014-38255964

http://www.slideshare.net/ccalypso/iscom-marketing-michel-augustin-dossier?next_slideshow=1

http://www.valeursdentrepreneurs.com/2015/03/12/le-management-selon-michel-de-rovira-une-forte-attention-portee-a-ses-salaries/

http://www.valeursdentrepreneurs.com/2015/03/12/le-management-selon-michel-de-rovira-une-forte-attention-portee-a-ses-salaries/

https://www.youtube.com/watch?v=jcPOmxLp77c

https://www.youtube.com/watch?v=Lbz30MjQP3k

https://www.youtube.com/watch?v=Lbz30MjQP3k

ANNEXES

1. PRODUCTS' RANGE: COOKIES

2. PRODUCTS' RANGE: TO GO

3. PRODUCTS' RANGE: APERITIVO BISCUITS

4. PRODUCTS' RANGE: JUICES

5. PRODUCTS' RANGE: SHARABLE DESSERTS

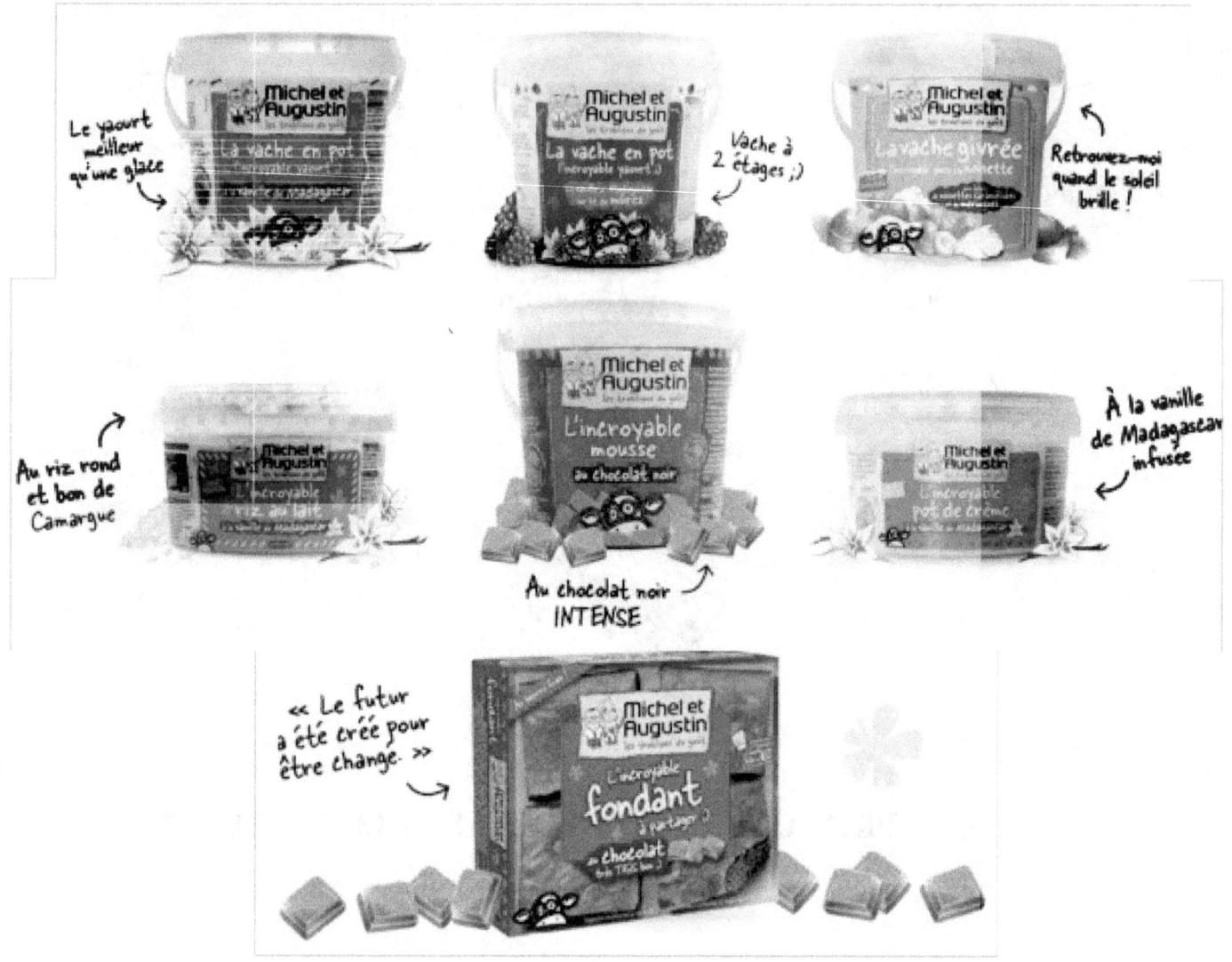

6. EXAMPLE OF PRODUCT SHEET

Chocolate ganache with 70% cacao

Delicious bits of hazelnut

Our "petites baguettes" side :)

What's in our petites baguettes?

A pure, crispy butter cookie, flour, sugar, real butter and a touch of honey.
Zero artificial colors. Zero preservatives.

7.   EXAMPLE OF RECIPE:

Our TORRID idea for delicious dessert

Delicately place a spoonful of yogurt in your cow cup*

with vanilla from Madagascar

with hazelnut

Crumble your petits cookies with 10 petits fingertips.. Sprinkle over your yogurt

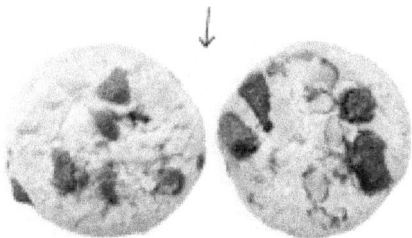

...add fresh fruit. Or don't

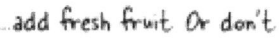
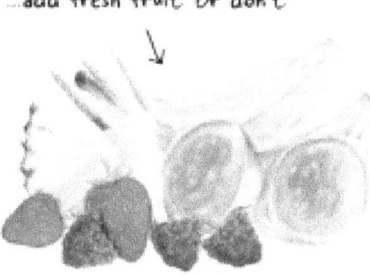

And voilà! 7 minutes late, right before your eyes, a REALLY delicious dessert!

* no cows harmed ;)

8. EXAMPLE OF STREET MARKETING OPERATIONS

9. TO KEEP IN MIND

It was in 2014, 2015 is off to a flying start!

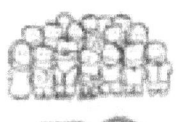
78 Kooks. (including)

4002 job applications received. (2 positions remain available).

3 Banana Farms
Paris - Lyon - NYC

3 pastry-certified graduation ceremonies.

21 Sales reps visit the biggest French cities, walking on their 2 feet, riding tricycles, driving kangoos, flying magic carpets.

An intense growth of **+44%**

that is to say
19 pastry-certified kooks (or almost certified).

1 Sold every single minute in France.

1 Sold every 10 seconds in the WORLD.

21 million creations enjoyed in the world.

MICHEL ET AUGUSTIN

www.ingramcontent.com/pod-product-compliance
Lightning Source LLC
Chambersburg PA
CBHW080819220526
45466CB00011BB/3614